Help!

To Jack Lemmon
with admiration
& more..

from
Mel Calman
X :)

1989

By the same author

Bed-Sit (*Jonathan Cape*)
Boxes (*Jonathan Cape*)
Calman & Women (*Jonathan Cape*)
My God (*Souvenir Press*)
The Penguin Calman
The New Penguin Calman
This Pestered Isle (*Times Newspapers Ltd*)
Couples (*The Workshop*)
Dr Calman's Dictionary of Psychoanalysis (*W. H. Allen*)
But it's my turn to leave you . . . (*Methuen*)
How about a little quarrel before bed? (*Methuen*)

Mel Calman

HELP!

and other ruminations

Methuen

First published in 1982 by
Methuen London Ltd
11 New Fetter Lane, London EC4P 4EE
Reprinted (twice) 1982

ISBN 0 413 50690 8

Printed in Great Britain
by Fletcher & Son Ltd, Norwich

These cartoons first appeared in *The Times* and *The Sunday Times*

To the Government – for making a middle-aged masochist happy . . .

I once had a brief and curious encounter with a customer. As well as my cartoon activities, I run a small gallery devoted to selling cartoon originals and graphics, and occasionally (in spite of the recession) we have customers. This particular customer, a charming, intelligent lady with a fine figure of a cheque book behind her, bought one of my cartoons. After expressing delight that I was the creator of this work of art, she asked: 'Did you do the caption as well?'

I was then torn between a desire to escort her to the door and a need to keep the cash flow flowing. 'Why do you ask?' 'Oh,' she said, 'I thought you might have stolen the idea from someone.'

I cite this bizarre exchange as a reason for writing this introduction. I feel I should stand up and try to explain what I do for a living.

I do not, for example, simply stay in bed all morning, merely to rise at three in the afternoon, bath, eat and steal a few jokes. *The Times* likes to see my gloomy face at some point in the day and my other clients need to have their faces washed and brightened by my presence in their lives. Here is how I work.

I get up about 8.30 am – reluctantly. I eat a small breakfast and shave a small portion of my face. I dress and drive to my studio. I look at the clutter of years of old drawings and magazines, and shudder. Must tidy all this tomorrow, I say to myself. I sharpen pencils, read my mail, put on some music, then go out for a second breakfast.

During the day I grapple with bits of advertising work, illustrate articles and think of jokes. At the end of the afternoon on four days of the week, I go to *The Times*. I consult the oracles about the choice of subject. There is nothing funny happening in the world. I try to find a fresh approach to same old problems. I read the papers, I listen to the radio, I even talk to journalists. I hope to find a joke lurking somewhere among the clutter of my desk and mind.

Jokes are about making unexpected connexions. They join up the invisible dots between two subjects. If they work, people laugh and if they don't, people seem to get annoyed. A dull article might still be informative, but an unfunny joke is irritating.

I never planned to be a cartoonist. It happened to me over the years, in the same way that one acquires a mortgage and grey hairs.

A professional cartoonist has to perform to order. You can have flu, the plague and dandruff in your soul, but the newspaper must go to press and editors are very reluctant to print a blank space on their front page.

And not only must you produce, you must produce something that makes other people laugh. After all these years, I still don't understand this strange mechanism. It is a bit like doing a crossword, where you know there must be a solution and all it needs is sweat and tearing up pieces of paper. And every once in a while, a good joke will pop into one's head like a golden bonus, and you can recognize it immediately as funny and, even better, true. I tend to prefer jokes which tell you something about people.

My jokes reflect my attitudes to life, which is why I cannot steal them from anyone else. I do not put on a cynical, pessimistic hat when considering the day's news and then go home to become a normal jolly person. I am a cynical pessimist who happens to be able to make and draw jokes. The gloom feeds my work, and I imagine that it is simply my good luck that this slant on life matches the mood of Britain today. In fact, events nowadays outstrip my wildest glooms. Who could have ever imagined Great Britain having over three million unemployed? What pessimist could invent such wholesale despair?

The problem for a cartoonist today is that he must read the news and still be able to laugh.

Meanwhile I will go and have another cup of tea so as to delay for another ten minutes the agony of trying to be funny. If you know of a good joke that I can steal, please send it to me in a plain brown envelope, c/o Methuen. Thank you.

Mel Calman

Of course we've come
a long way since
those days of economies
and shortages...

Festival
of
Britain-
25yrs...

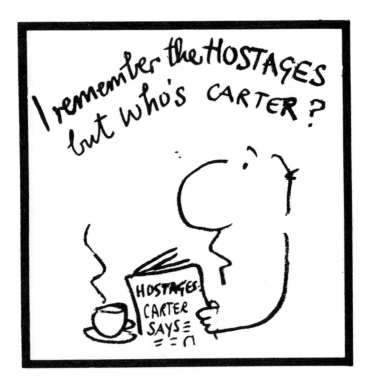

Nobody's perfect..
REAGAN SPEAKS

Reagan deserves an award for BEST performance under fire..
OSCAR AWARDS
000

Things must be really desperate..
BL
VOTE
TO
WORK

How Un-British!
"WE, WONT STRIKE"
SAY OILMEN.

Do you want to be delayed by road, rail or sea?
HOLS 81
HOLS 81.
No dear- last year we were delayed at LUTON - 1978 was when we were hijacked..

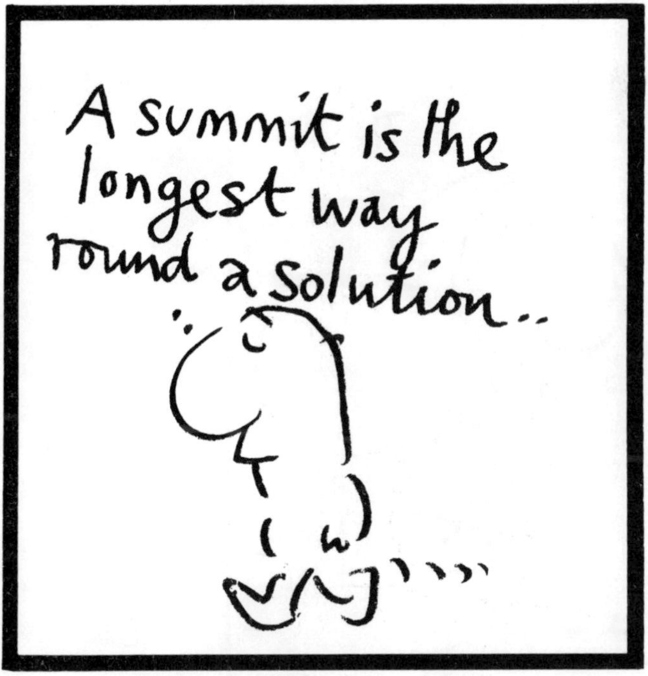
A summit is the longest way round a solution..

A is for ARSON
B is for BOMBS
C is for CS Gas..
ABC for 1981.

TICK!
TICK!

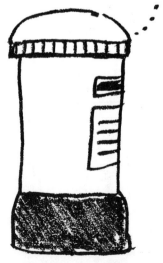

Couldn't you mug me when I can get an ambulance?

We need a bomb that only KILLS the people who drop it..
Neutron Bomb go-ahead

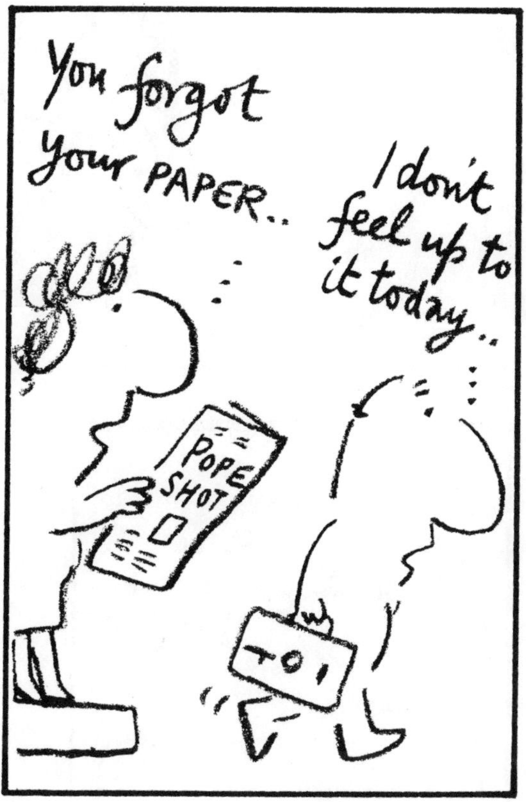
You forgot your PAPER..
I don't feel up to it today..
POPE SHOT

My economic strategy will be to emigrate..

CUTS

Spare 50p. to cash a cheque?

This per cent can't manage on 4 per cent...

Just as well you didn't win any yesterday, isn't it?
POUND LOW

We can afford to get into debt again...
MLR DOWN

You can now read Economies at Cambridge..
CAREERS

Doctor - I've got 'Price - Watcher's Neck.'

It's a great BUDGET if you don't want to enjoy living..

Not mine..
SPIRITS UP!

The Clichés are bang on target..
Budget News

But, dear boy—
we were counting
on you betraying
us..

Don't worry, Prime Minister - the head of the K.G.B works for us..
M.I5

Who's sponsoring your boycott?

If there's no GAMES - what will we do for boredom in the evenings?
SPORT & SPORT

I badly need a pair of rose-coloured spectacles..
Cheaper GLASSES

NO NO!
IM LEFT!
NO- YOU'RE RIGHT!
I'M LEFT OF LEFT!!
YOU'RE TOO SELF-CENTRED TO BE LEFT!
I feel left out...

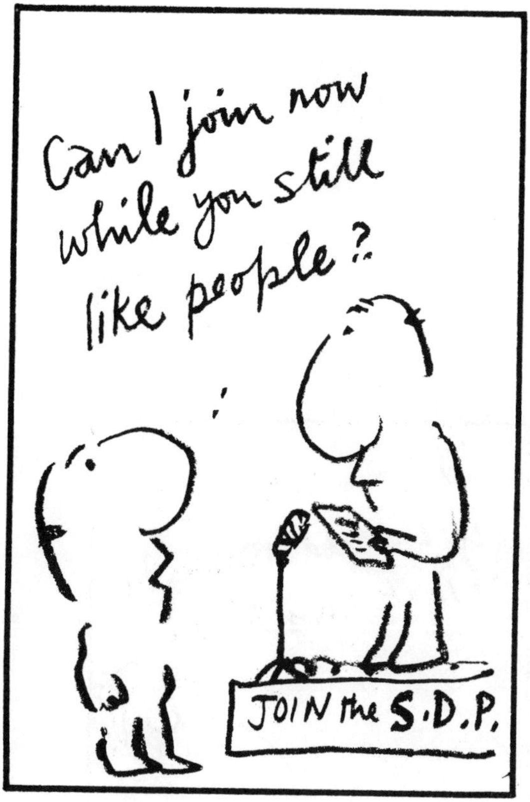
Can I join now while you still like people?
JOIN the S.D.P.

Will that stop the speeches being full of HOT air?
TUC BANS SMOKING

At last! A politician who knows whether he's coming or going ..
JIM QUITS

What kind of Labour Party allows that to happen?
LEFT WINS.

I can't vote LABOUR now it's gone Left...

How moderately exciting!
MODERATE ALLIANCE GOES AHEAD!

I find all this intellectual theorising rather highbrow..
SUCKS! YAH!! YAROO!!
Deputy Leader CONTEST

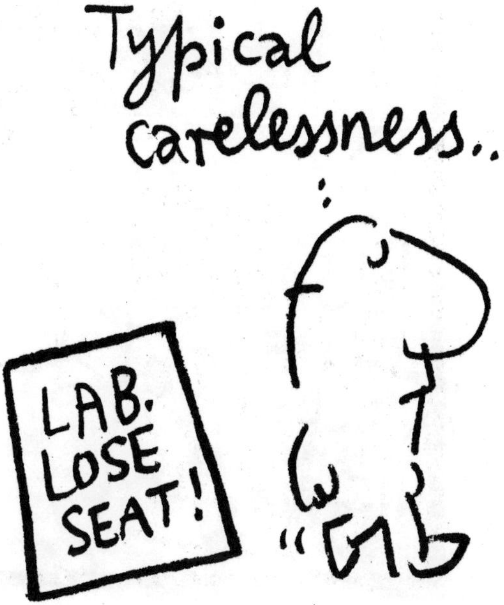

Typical carelessness..
LAB. LOSE SEAT!

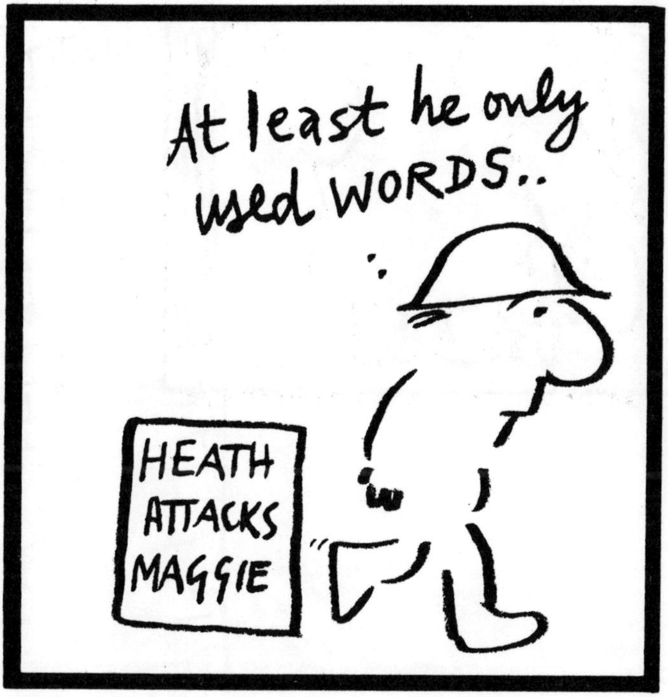
At least he only used WORDS..
HEATH ATTACKS MAGGIE

If someone hit MAGGIE with a steel chair, the chair would collapse..

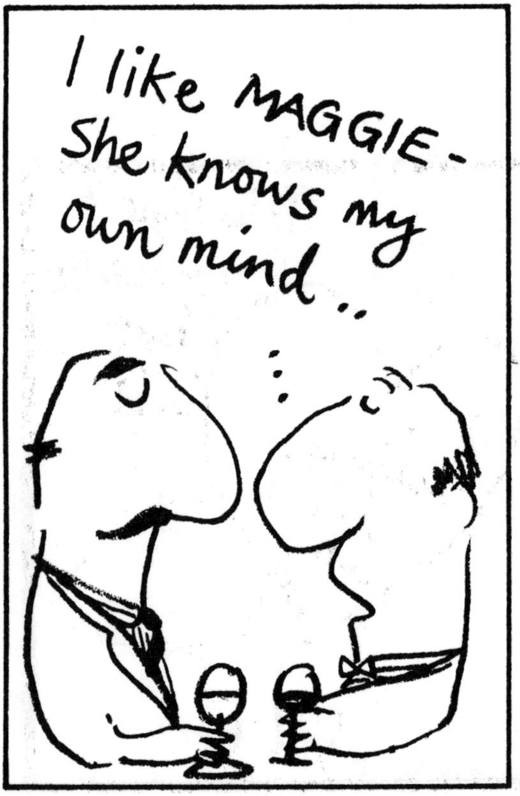
I like MAGGIE - She knows my own mind ..

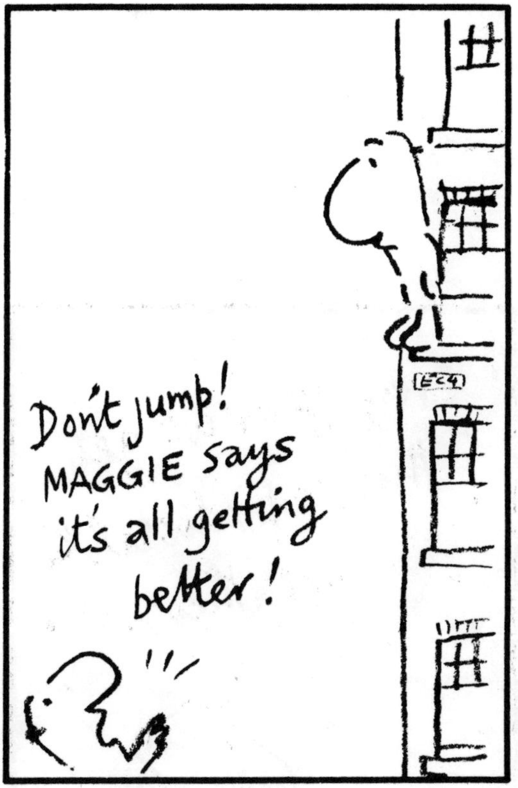
EC4
Don't jump! MAGGIE says it's all getting better!

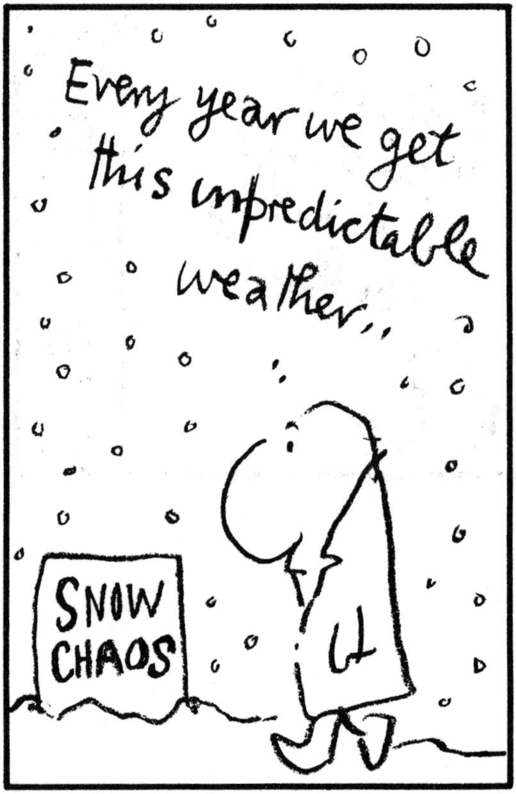
Every year we get this unpredictable weather..
SNOW CHAOS

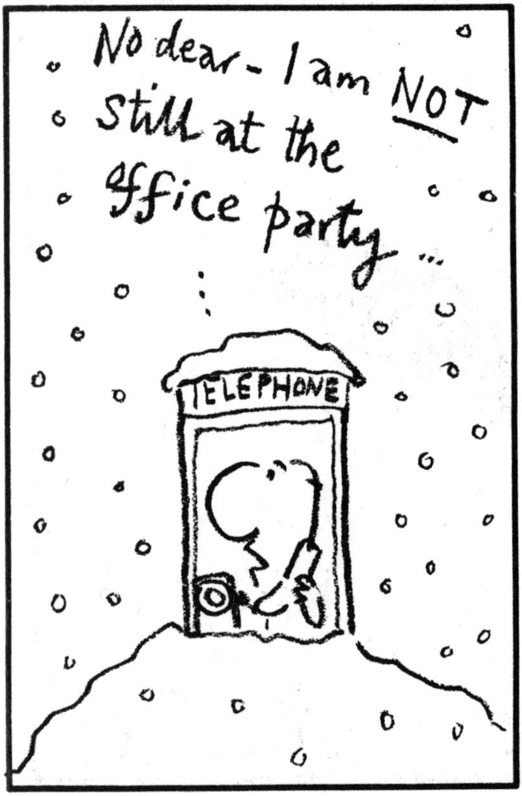
No dear - I am NOT still at the office party ...
TELEPHONE

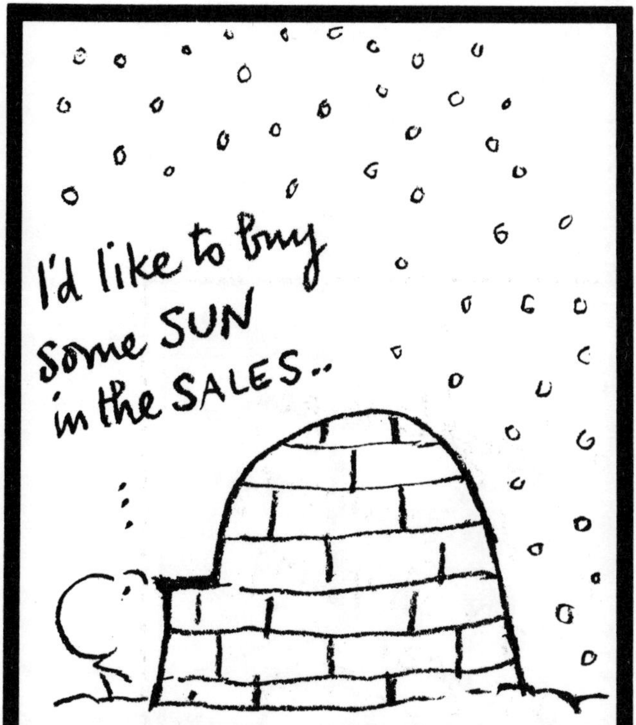
I'd like to buy
some SUN
in the SALES..

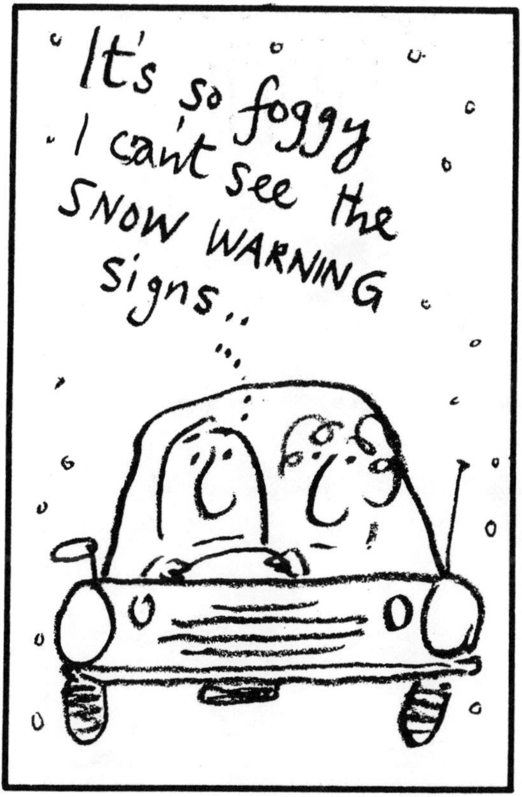
It's so foggy I can't see the SNOW WARNING signs..

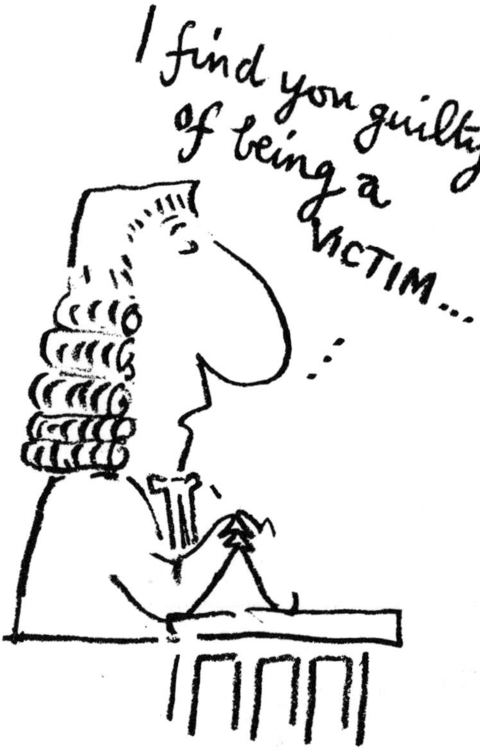
I find you guilty of being a VICTIM...

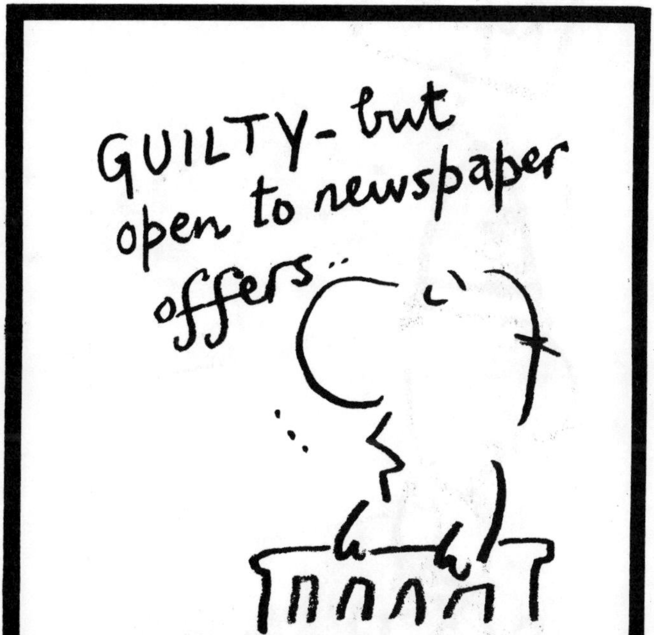
GUILTY - but
open to newspaper
offers...

And then, your Honour, I tripped over some insufficient evidence..

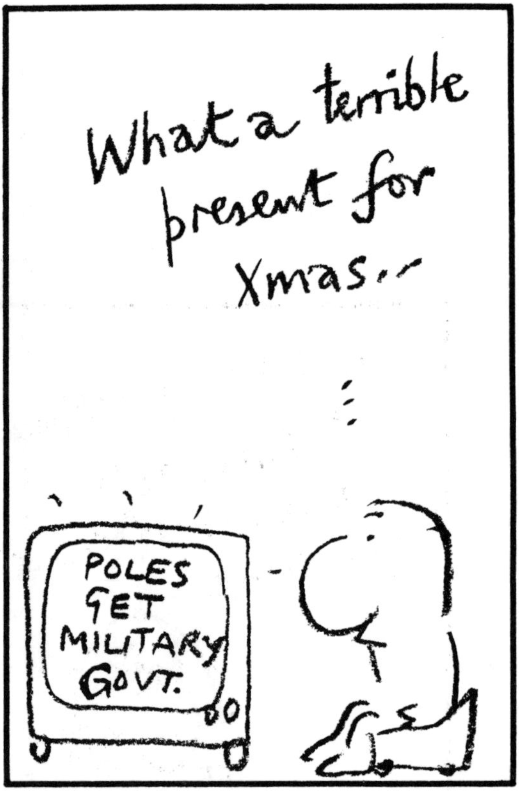
What a terrible present for Xmas..
POLES GET MILITARY GOVT.

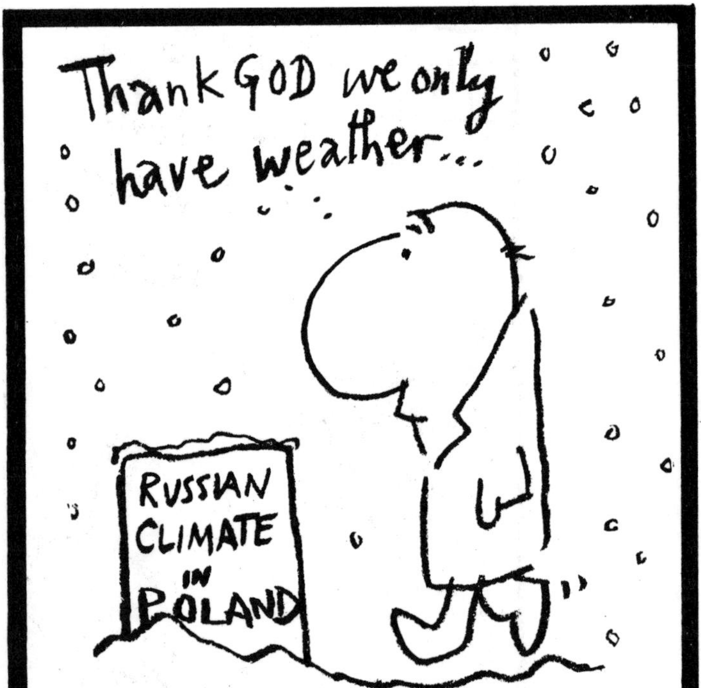
Thank GOD we only have weather...
RUSSIAN CLIMATE IN POLAND

The question is-
will they invade
or will they only
intervene?
RUSSIA
&
POLAND

There is, of course, no Russian word for 'INVASION'
RUSSIAN LANGUAGE BBC2

A pound of sausages - the ones with no income tax in them..
£1.00
£4
£

We've got a strange Iranian student - he never gets deported..

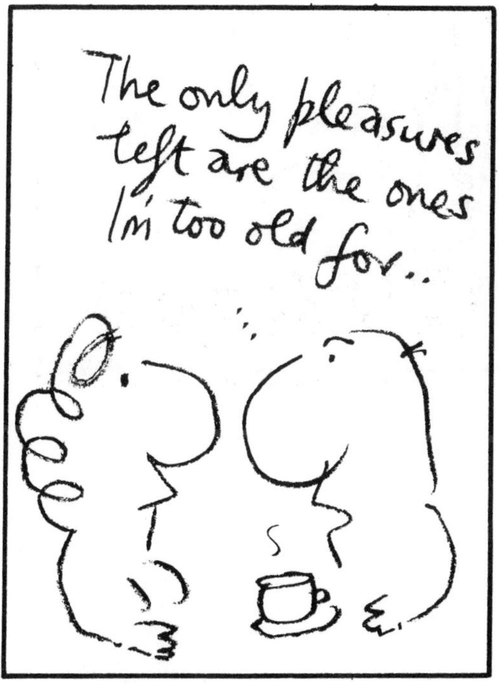
The only pleasures left are the ones I'm too old for...

My colleague is away - having his bureaucracy removed...
ADMINISTRATOR

Are there only 2 shopping days left for me to forget to buy you something?

Tell me something cheerful - even if it's about Barbara Cartland..
THE SUTCLIFFE TRIAL
SANDS

Will you be able to support a second wife in the style to which your first wife is accustomed?

I could now BUY a house - if I wasn't BUYING a missile..
MORTGAGES CHEAPER!

That's one way to get this country back on its feet again..
NO TRAINS.

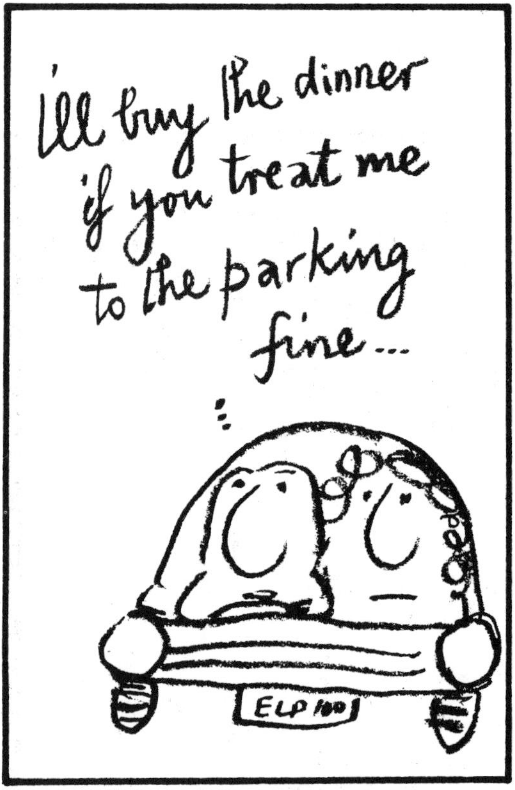
I'll buy the dinner if you treat me to the parking fine...
ELP 100

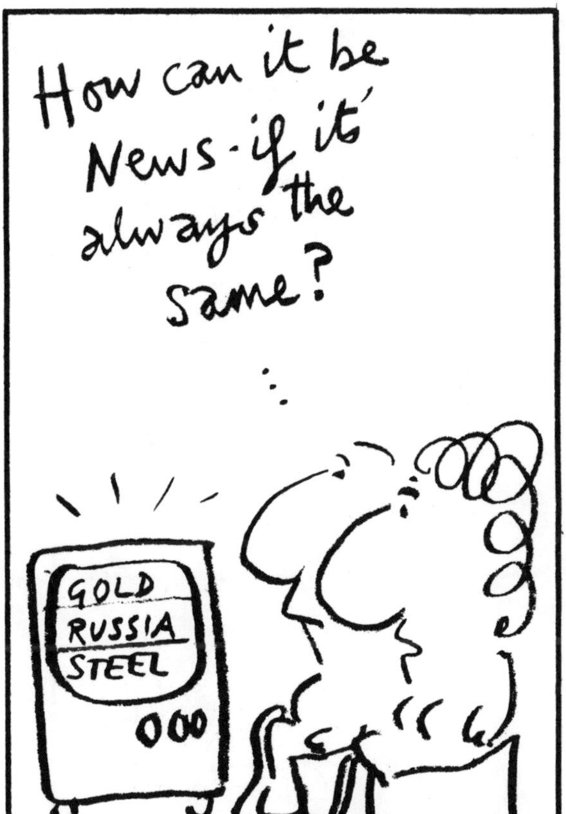
How can it be News - if it's always the same?
GOLD
RUSSIA
STEEL

I suppose 1st. Class CITIZENS will be allowed to live abroad...
...
3 CLASS CITIZENS..
PHONES UP!
LEB DEARER!

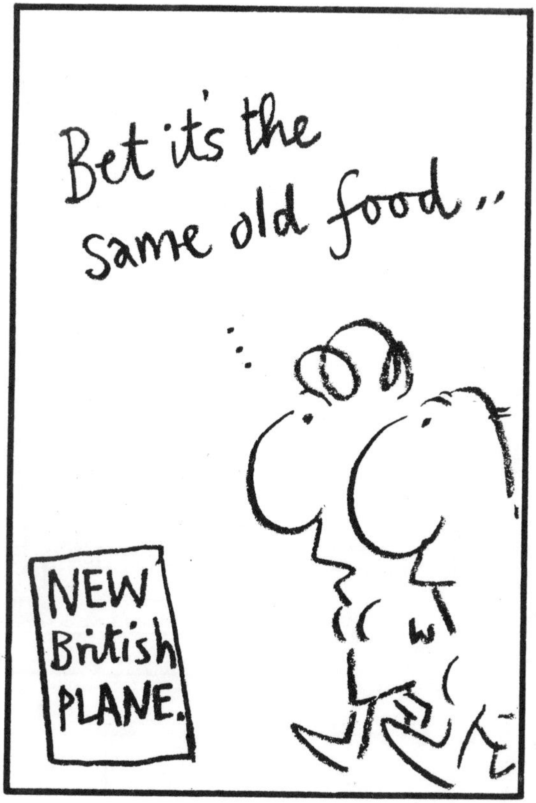
Bet it's the same old food..
NEW British PLANE.

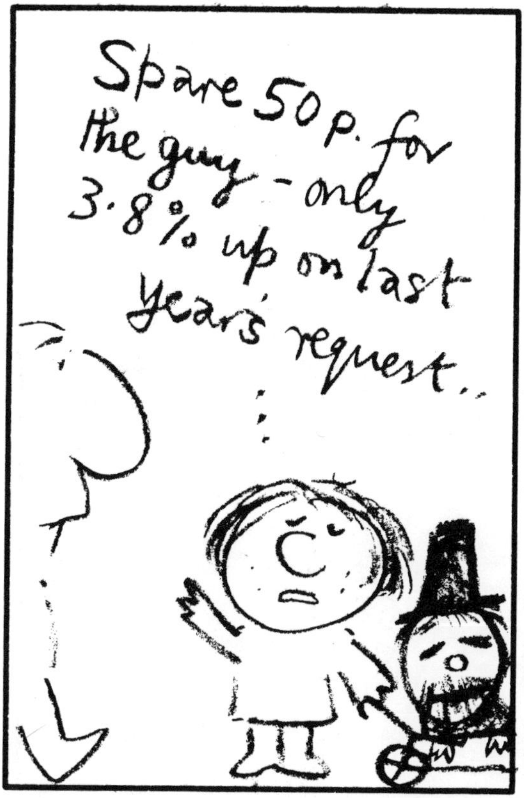
Spare 50p. for the guy - only 3.8% up on last year's request...

If I hang on much longer — the price will have gone up again..

I once wrote to the Post Office complaining but it never arrived..

Where else can a masochist go for Christmas?
NO SAILINGS TO N.IRELAND
TRAVEL AGENT

No-one is going to give you a JOB while you look like a politician..
JOB CENTRE

I hear the Economy is moving in the right direction..
DOLE Queue

By the time I'd found this present, I'd forgotten who I was buying it for...
HAPPY XMAS

One day everyone loves you – the next you're unemployed..

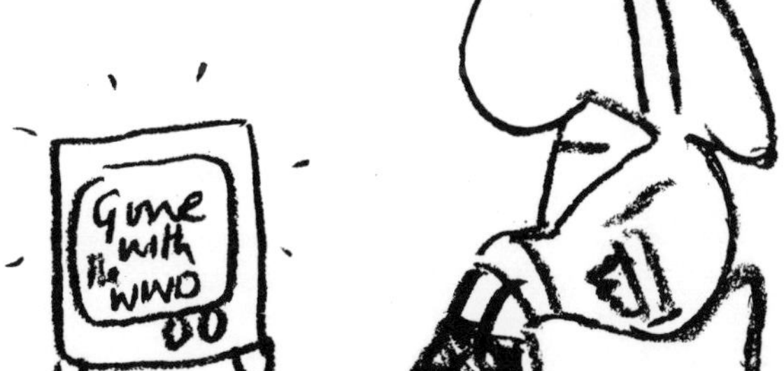